SOARING

By Mary Ann Hannon

and

Dr. Jeri Fink

SOARING

By Mary Ann Hannon and Dr. Jeri Fink

Published by Book Web Publishing, LTD
Book Web Minis
All rights reserved
Copyright 2018

Original and modified cover art by D Sharon Pruitt and CoverDesignStudio.com

ISBN-13: 978-1-941882-25-2

Edited by Donna Paltrowitz, BS, MS, Certified Reading and Education Specialist, Author

To Pat, Ricky, and Stu - our best friends and husbands

and

to our children and grandchildren

Read cutting-edge Book Web Minis

Why SOARING? **Meet Mary Ann Hannon**

I have spent years studying and applying the new approach to Psychology known as "Positive Psychology." Positive Psychology looks at what is right with us while traditional psychology focuses more on what is wrong with us.

I'm fascinated by the power of these ideas in daily life and how they can greatly impact well-being. They're simple and easy to use. When "practiced" you can improve physical and psychological health, boost your well-being, and be happier!

This book looks at some of the well-researched areas and practices that can send us Soaring!

Mary Ann Hannon is a New York State Certified School Psychologist who has spent her professional life in the service of children, families, and communities. In that position, she also served as a Parent Advocate for Children with Disabilities and held numerous workshops and seminars on ADHD, Eating Disorders, and Therapeutic Interventions for Grief and Loss. She has worked as an Adjunct Professor in Psychology at Molloy College and trained with the Nassau Medical Reserve Corps where she received a Certificate in Disaster Response. Ongoing study and research has always been a big part of her life. She holds a Certificate in the relatively new area of Positive Psychology which explores the scientific study of human strengths and virtues. The goal of this innovative approach is to explore how humans can live with dignity and purpose; emphasizing and strengthening positive character traits such as compassion, creativity, empathy and resilience while increasing the presence of mindfulness and well-being.

Why Book Web Publishing?

Book Web Publishing produces original mini books in e-book and print formats. If you're interested in doing a mini book check out our website, www.bookwebminis.com and contact us.

Dr. Jeri Fink is an author, photographer, and family therapist/clinical social worker. She has worked in mental health and written over 30 nonfiction and fiction books for adults and children. Her articles and blogs appear on and offline, including hundreds of topics ranging from psychology, technology, fiction, humor, to family. She wrote the *Broken Series* – seven thrillers set in the 15th century to the present. In the *Book Web Minis Series* she explores cutting-edge nonfiction that affirms the power of positive meaning in life.

Donna Paltrowitz began her career as a NYC teacher and licensed reading specialist determined to teach children to enjoy reading. Her path evolved into developing, editing, and authoring more than 100 published children's books, adult books, computer books, magazine articles, and educational software. Her interests range from property management, positive psychology, and spirituality. In the *Book Web Minis Series*, she explores new paths to affirm positive energy, giving a voice to new discoveries, expert insights, and innovators.

SOARING

CONTENTS

Introduction
The Seven Steps to Soaring

Introduction

Are you happy?

SOARING means learning to be joyful, discovering delight at your fingertips, and finding meaning in what you do. It's about thinking positively and being mindful of the present – getting in touch with the real you.

SOARING is about finding happiness in yourself, the people around you, and your world.

What do the experts say? A recent Harris Poll found that only one in three Americans reported being happy. The Life Twist study, commissioned by American Express, concluded that Americans are redefining success and happiness in a way that doesn't involve wealth. There's more to happiness than how much you earn and the size of your home. 83% of the people in the study called themselves a "work in progress."

Each of the following chapters focus on one aspect of SOARING, guiding you to achieve the confidence, enthusiasm, and happiness that you deserve.

Let's go SOARING!

The Seven Steps to Soaring

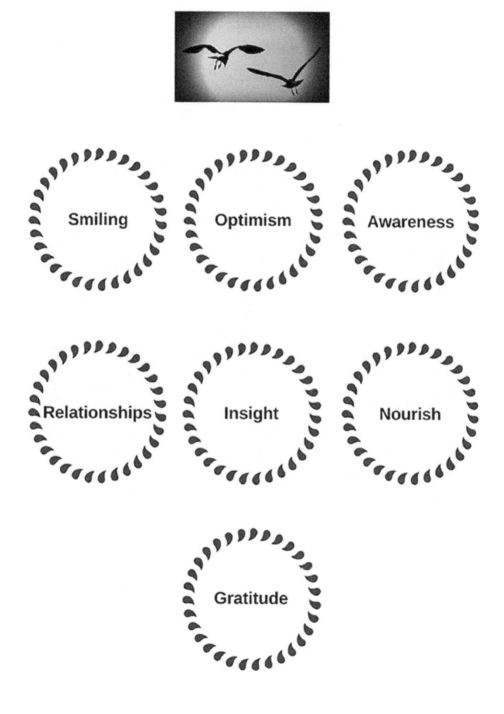

Smiling

Optimism

Awareness

Relationships

Insight

Nourish

Gratitude

1

S miling

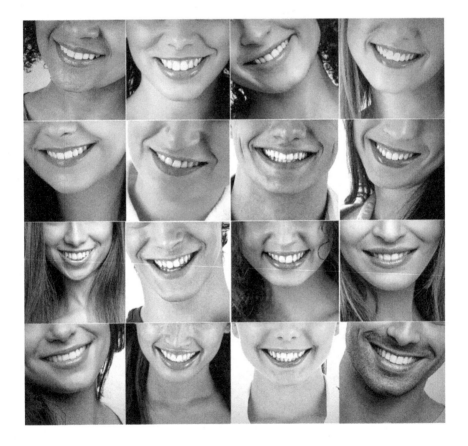

Do you have a spare .03 seconds?

That's all it takes to smile. I smile a lot because it makes me SOAR.

The New York State Psychological Association gave me an award for my research on the effects of smiling. Smiling reduces stress, sends positive messages, and is contagious. Famous smiles like Mona Lisa, Mickey and Minnie Mouse, and The Cheshire Cat are unforgettable. Even babies "smile" in the womb, as if practicing. By 6 weeks old those babies are trading smiles with everyone around them.

Take a look at this baby. Does she make you smile?

The brain is wired to see smiling as a positive. Here's how it works. When someone smiles with you at a party, from a screen, or in a marketing campaign, they give off positive feelings. Studies have shown that whether it's Face Book or a stranger on the street, a smile triggers feel-good emotions. That's a lot of power in .03 seconds.

The power of a smile.

You have the power to make yourself and someone feel good almost instantly. What a gift!

Smiling is wildly contagious. In other words, you can quickly change a bad moment into a good one; a negative into a positive. It's quick, easy, and takes little or no effort. A recent study found that when people are shown photos of happy, smiling faces, and told to frown, they couldn't do it. They *had* to smile back.

If you smile at others they can't help but return the favor.

Can you smile at this story? I was working on this book in a local diner. I glanced over at a stranger in another booth. He was sitting alone, looking very sad. I caught his eye and smiled. For a tiny moment he was unsure. Then he couldn't stop himself – he smiled back. The smile spread across his entire face; it changed his body language; he sat straighter, squared his shoulders, and held his head higher. Grinning, I went over and explained what I was doing.

We both laughed!

> A smile is a curve that sets everything straight.
>
> *Phyllis Diller, actress and comedienne, 1917-2012*

Consider three ways smile power affects people.

First impressions: It takes as little as seven seconds to form a first impression - and first impressions last. There's an old saying, "you never get a second chance to make a first impression." Numerous studies found that first impressions are stable and hard to change. What does that have to do with smiling power? If you're meeting a colleague, potential date, or group member, smile and they'll feel good about themselves and the new person in their lives. Frown and . . . you can fill in the words.

Business and sales: There's a common rule in sales – offer a killer smile. It's one of the first things a salesperson learns, along with being a people person. A smile puts customers at ease, looks natural, and makes you seem likable. Ask yourself these questions. Would you buy a new car from a salesman who is smiling or from one who is snarling? Would you trust someone to sell you a computer when they're frowning? Would you hire an employee who looks angry?

Dialing and smiling: Telemarketers are often told to smile when they give their pitch. The smile can be "heard" in their voice. These days most people don't care whether a telemarketer is smiling, but the concept holds. When you're speaking to a new person, trying to make an appointment or reservation, hoping to convince someone to vote a particular way, or just talking with a friend, smile and it will be heard in your voice.

Make your future brighter

There are many ongoing studies about smiling, facial expressions, attractiveness . . . the list is very long. One of the most interesting was by University of California, Berkley Researchers, LeeAnn Harker and Dacher Keltner. They looked at the smiles of students in their old yearbook photos and compared them to their well-being *30 years later*. Measuring the photo smiles, the researchers could predict marital success, well-being, and general happiness. "People photograph each other with casual ease and remarkable frequency," Harker and Keltner concluded, "usually unaware that each snapshot may capture as much about the future as it does the passing emotions of the moment."

A subsequent study of baseball card photos found that player's smile could predict their lifespan. Players with big smiles lived an average of 9 years longer.

Maybe it's time to think of smiling as part of healthy living – along with exercise, wholesome food, and relaxation.

Smile more!

You need to smile more. The average person smiles 20 times a day. Kick up the number. There will be new opportunities. Make it a habit to smile more and you and everyone around you will be happier.

Below are a few ways to develop the habit of smiling.

*Smile at the cashier in the supermarket and at other shoppers.

*Smile at your bus or cab driver, the train conductor, and the airline stewardess.

*Smile at co-workers, especially when they're having a bad day.

*Smile at your waiter or waitress.

*Smile at the gas station attendant.

*Smile at your neighbor.

*Smile at the repair people that come into your home.

*Smile at the receptionist.

*Smile at your hairdresser.

*Smile at the people behind the counter.

*Smile at your friends.

*Smile at and with your family and loved ones.

Write down other places where you can add a smile.

Anatomy of a Smile

What happens in your brain when you smile?

Smiling activates neural messages in your brain that benefit your health and happiness. It's accomplished through a neurotransmitter or chemical messenger that moves between nerve fibers, transferring signals from one cell to another. They're critical in everyday life and functions, affecting everything from telling your heart to beat to emotional responses.

The "feel good" neurotransmitter is called *dopamine*

When you smile, dopamine is released. It can relax your body, lower your heart rate, and reduce your blood pressure.

In other words, a smile goes a very long way!

Smiling in The Cloud

There are so many ways to smile in the cloud.
Check out a few below.

2

Optimism

Optimism. We all know what it *is* yet have a tough time finding an exact definition. Some people see it as looking through rose-colored glasses. Others ask the question – is the glass half full or half empty?

Optimism is looking at the glass and believing it *can* be full. It's a way of thinking based on hope, confidence in the future, success, and expecting the best.

Even when the moment doesn't look very good, optimists are sure that tomorrow will work out.

Drama Critic George Jean Nathan said it best:

An optimist is a fellow who believes a housefly is looking for a way to get out.

Optimists love good humor.

Choices

You have lots of choices. For example, imagine it's dinner time.

You and a friend have been busy all day. Now you're starving. Burgers sound great but all the best places have long waits and you don't have reservations.

A new gourmet burger restaurant just opened nearby but there are no reviews and you don't know anyone who has been there. The good news is that you won't have to wait for a table.

"Let's try it," you say optimistically. "It's probably very good."

"No," your friend quickly replies. "It's too new – let's wait until we know more about it."

You end up with a slice of pizza for dinner.

Optimism and pizza are choices

Maybe that burger would have been a lot better than pizza. You'll never know because you chose to be safe (or negative) not optimistic.

Optimism is a decision – a choice or habit about how to think. Instead of expecting doom and gloom (and bad hamburgers) you can *choose* hope, possibilities, and the belief that things will change.

It all depends on your attitude.

What does an optimistic attitude look like?

History has shown us over and over again that we need to believe; bad can be changed into good; ugly can become beautiful; and problems can be solved. Think *Cinderella* and *Beauty and the Beast*. We love those stories along with all happy endings.

It's a lot more fun to be happy and hopeful than sad and gloomy.

Look at the following statements. What makes them optimistic?

WHAT DOES OPTIMISM LOOK LIKE?

I buy a lottery ticket because I'm going to win mega millions.

I'll catch a fish from the dock and cook it for dinner.

I know the doctor will give me a good report. I can handle anything.

I make a good impression on interviews and always get the job.

I know my favorite baseball team will win. I know my dreams will come true.

I see the future as bright and full of sunshine. I believe that everyone will SOAR.

Each statement is positive; shows a belief in something good. It's upbeat, fun, and a great way to think about life.

However, everyone can't win the lottery, catch a fish for dinner, or get the job in an interview even though it's uplifting to *think* that way. Circumstances beyond your control can affect real life. A nasty neighbor moves next door. You catch the flu even though you had the flu shot. You get laid off because your company is closing even though you worked hard and did a good job.

Optimism doesn't deny that life throws you curve balls. The key is to think positive; be hopeful because things DO change; and if possible, recognize that you may have the power to make them change.

I call it optimism with a dose of reality!

Do

> I can't change the direction of the wind, but I can adjust my sails to always reach my destination.
>
> *Jimmy Dean, country music singer, actor, businessman, 1928-2010*

you want to be happier, more successful, live longer, and have less stress?

Research has proven that the habit of optimistic thinking makes you feel better about yourself. One Harvard study found that optimists were healthier than pessimists; cancer treatment has demonstrated the "power of positive thinking" in recovery; and optimistic athletes performed better than pessimists.

Making lemonade out of lemons *works*.

According to Dr. Martin Seligman, Psychologist and author of *Learned Optimism*, sports tells us a lot about the "playing field" when it comes to optimism. He found three "basic predictions" for sports performance. They apply to your life as well.

1. Optimists will win because they "try harder, particularly after defeat or under stiff challenge.

2. The same goes for teams – the more optimistic a team, the more likely they'll win.

3. When negative thinking is shifted into positive, people "win more."

What does that say about you and how you think?

The key is that it's all *within your power*. In real life things are not always sunny. Bad things DO happen to good people. It's natural and normal to be drawn into negativity.

Why do you have negative thoughts?

We're constantly thinking – our heads are full of endless chatter. Most of it is useless, unimportant, and passes through quickly. According to the National Science Foundation we have at least 50,000 thoughts a day.

Dr. Raj Raghunathan, in *Psychology Today,* writes that up to 70% of this daily "mental chatter" is mostly negative.

Why?

Your brain is wired to pay more attention to negatives rather than positives. It's safer – and normal. Look at it this way. As cavemen, negativity was built into the brain so we could survive by avoiding danger. Suspicion prevented early humans from wandering into dangerous, unknown caves or trusting potentially aggressive strangers. We needed it to stay alive.

You can say the same thing about life today. If you're *too* positive, *too* trusting, you can find yourself in big trouble. Think walking down a dark city alley in the middle of the night or trusting aggressive scammers.

Studies by Dr. John Cacioppo at Ohio State University, found that our brains respond more to negative than positive news. As with the cavemen, it's safer. The difference is that today it's more psychological than physical. When you think the worst you can't lose. If things go bad you say, "I knew that was going to happen." If things go well, you call it "luck."

People take advantage of this built-in negative bias. Politicians rant about the awful qualities of their opponents. Newscasts feature criminals and psychopaths before Good Samaritans and success stories. Gossip and rumors focus on shocking secrets and bad behaviors not on kind, generous individuals.

When you view life as negative - live and think in shadows that affect everything from having a good time to winning a tennis game, the world looks darker. Pessimists explain positive events as lucky and temporary, believing the world is basically bad and evil will prevail over good. According to *Psychology Today*, pessimists have higher blood pressure, more cynicism, and are more susceptible to depression.

Imagine it's holiday season and you celebrate by gorging on glazed ham, buttered roast potatoes, and eggnog cheesecake. When the holidays are over you're terrified to get on the scale. Part of you says, why stop? Everything tastes so good. Another part argues that you should go back to healthy living. You know, a devil and an angel sitting on your shoulders?

That's negative fighting positive thoughts - the caveman inside you. You can go SOARING by changing your habit, attitude, and style of thinking; being aware of the negativity bias; and becoming an optimist with a dose of reality!

In other words, you can see the holiday as being fun and indulgent but now it's time to get back to real life.

The idea of optimism and positive thinking has been around a long time. Epictetus, the ancient stoic philosopher born in A.D. 55, wisely wrote in *The Art of Living:*

Your happiness depends on three things, all of which are within your power: your will, your ideas concerning the events in which you are involved, and the use you make of your ideas.

Consider one of the most famous, and determined woman in history. Helen Keller lived a long life from 1880-1968. She overcame crippling limitations of being both deaf and blind to become a famous author, lecturer, and activist.

Helen Keller, 1904

Library of Congress LC-USZ62-112513

"Optimism is the faith that leads to achievement."

The world is filled with optimistic people who overcame obstacles that seemed insurmountable. Think about Jim Abbott, the Major League Baseball pitcher born without a right hand who pitched over 800 strikeouts in his baseball career. Franklin D. Roosevelt, one of the country's most beloved Presidents, had polio and spent much of his life in a wheel chair. Stevie Wonder, one of the most famous singers and musicians, was born blind.

They were optimists who believed they could overcome their disabilities. What about you?

How to change your thinking style.

"Habits of thinking need not be forever," according to Dr. Martin Seligman. "One of the most significant findings in psychology in the last twenty years is that individuals can choose the way they think."

How?

The way to change is practice – making positive thinking a habit. You'll develop a new attitude. People around you will sense the change and respond more positively to you. It's a personal decision. For many, negative thinking has become a habit. You *can learn* how to be optimistic.

Learning and practicing optimism will change your life. Give it a try. You have nothing to lose and everything to gain.

The following suggestions will lead to a healthier, happier, and more optimistic view on life . . . with a dose of reality.

Get up in the morning and set a goal to do something you enjoy. It can be big or small - take a walk, see a movie, call a special friend.

Make a list of things you're looking forward to doing.

Pick something that's routine and change it into a positive.

Take a photo of a happy moment or scene that brings good thoughts.

Visualize a memory or person that makes you feel happy and optimistic.

Listen to others talk about positive experiences.

Relax and listen to your favorite music.

Share with others your positive experiences.

Try something new and upbeat.

Listen to the news, know what's going on in the world, but don't overdo it! Negativity is often king in news reporting.

Search for stories, movies, and televsion about feel-good things and experiences.

Be wary of people, politicians, and businesspeople who focus only on the negative.

Laugh - it's contagious!

Optimism in The Cloud

Be kind to others

Share good news

Avoid bad news

Don't make negative posts

Retweet, post, or forward happy stories

**Keep a list of blogs, networks, and websites
that are helpful, inspiring, and optimistic**

Invite optimists to be your friends and followers

Praise others

Be polite and respectful

Celebrate differences

Ignore trolls (people who fight online)

3

Art of Living

What is the Art of Living?

The Art of Living is the creative expression of who you are, what you love, and your vision of the good life. It's a simple concept - a perfectly baked apple pie, a landscape painted in your garage, or a speech to motivate co-workers. Maybe it's a flawless business plan, a beautifully decorated home, or a thriving garden. It's not just the end product but the process – the creativity it took to get there.

Many of us don't realize – or utilize – the talents and abilities we have. Some people fear the word "creativity." How can a person who draws stick figures be an artist in the kitchen? How can someone who thinks in numbers be creative? How can a manager who skillfully handles a staff be an empathetic friend?

The answer is simple. You're the artist of your life. It's about who you are, not the mindsets of people who don't get it. Maybe the person who draws stick figures can prepare gourmet French food. The individual who thinks in numbers may be be a gifted canasta player. The manager who directs his staff may be a talented party planner.

Life is full of joy. You find happiness, pleasure, connections, and great experiences. You also find sadness, struggle, and frustration. No one is immune to the ups and downs of daily life. It's how you deal with it that counts.

A world of choices lies within you. You have talents, dreams, and creativity. You may not be a famous actor, dazzling fashionista, or Wall Street mogul. It doesn't matter. What you *can be* is an artist that sculpts your own life, designs your happiness, and draws love and peace from those around you.

The Art of Living is the creative expression of who you are, what you love, and your vision of the good life. It's a simple concept - a perfectly baked apple pie, a landscape painted in your garage, or a speech to motivate co-workers. Maybe it's a flawless business plan, a beautifully decorated home, or a thriving garden. It's not just the end product but the process – the creativity it took to get there.

Creativity in the Art of Living

We all have it. Too often, we call creativity by different names. Maybe you say you have a "knack" for training dogs or an "eye" for selecting clothes. Others might notice that you have a talent or skill in carpentry – even though you work in a business office. Some might comment that you missed your calling in life.

Here's the truth - you didn't miss your calling or have some secret talent. It has always been inside you. The desire to create something beautiful, show your inner vision, and share the results is very much alive. You may not have the talent or skill to fill a theater, cook for people in a gourmet restaurant, or write a novel, but that doesn't mean you're not creative. It's there and has always been there – *inside* where you feel it.

Expressing your creativity brings a precious gift called well-being.

Scribbles

Visual art (and well-being) starts with scribbles.

Toddlers make random, colorful crayon marks on paper. Scribbles take on more meaning as the child grows. Shapes appear at 3-4 years old and stick figures magically join the artwork. Usually stick figures represent people a child knows and loves – mom, dad, siblings, family, pets, and friends.

Whether scribbles or stick figures, happy suns or pets, you love and praise kids art. That's because you know the child is showing true feelings. They don't have to be great artists – the kids are simply expressing joyful creativity. When you applaud the kids they feel good and you feel good – sharing a positive moment.

Creativity and well-being

Whether you're making a wood carving, running a road race, or teaching a child how to ride a bike, your creativity builds well-being. What tastes better – the tomato you bought at the supermarket or the one grown lovingly by a neighbor? What feels better – the beaded bracelet purchased online or the one made by a child just for you? What's more fun – jamming in a band with your buddies or listening to music on your headphones?

Research has repeatedly proven that there is a powerful relationship between creativity and well-being:

*Doing a creative activity just *once a day* can lead to a more positive view of the world. Tamlin, Conner, DeYoung & Paul found that creativity and well-being go hand-in-hand.

*Creativity fosters a positive psychological outlook. Perach & Wisman concluded that creativity is an affirmation of life.

*Creating or working hands-on can be an antidote to technology and improve mental health and happiness. According to Dr. Kelly Lambert, Chief of the Lambert Behavioral Neuroscience Laboratory at the University of Richmond, when we use our hands, repair, or create something it makes us feel more alive.

How do you get there? Needs in the Art of Living

People have basic needs that must be met to reach their creative potential. These needs overlap in our lives; they move through different stages, ages, and lifestyles. When satisfied, our needs inspire us to actively express our creativity.

Our basic needs are biological – air, food, water, and shelter. When those needs are met we look for protection from the elements, safety, and security.

Securing the basics frees us to think about personal, emotional, and psychological needs. Love, belonging, friendchip, intimacy, and community become more important, along with self-esteem, confidence, and respect for and by others. Satisfying our needs brings us to a comfort zone where we can celebrate what we have and let our creativity blossom.

Dr. Abraham Maslow, 1908-1970

Dr. Maslow was an American psychologist *and* optimist who viewed people in terms of their needs. Maslow focused on what goes right in human behavior and potential rather than what goes wrong.

He believed in a motivational theory where people work to meet basic needs and then reach for higher ones. Maslow drew a triangle called *The Hierarchy of Needs* to show how human needs are prioritized, starting with lower needs, through psychological needs, to the highest level, self-awareness or as Maslow called it, self-actualization.

Maslow, often known as the "father of humanistic psychology," studied the best and brightest people in history, concluding that the "more we learn about man's natural tendencies, the easier it will be to tell him how to be good, how to be happy."

"The key question," Maslow said, "isn't 'What fosters creativity?' But why in God's name isn't everyone creative?"

The Art of Living in the 21st Century

Today's world is a lot smaller than the days of creative explorers searching for new lands and inventors figuring out how to build a horseless carriage. Now we look for planets, galaxies, and tiny quantum particles. Our most creative scientists work to prove the existence of multiuniverses and the nature of human life; our most creative philosophers explore the connection between artificial intelligence and human thought.

Earth has shrunk virtually – we're connected globally and interpersonally in ways never seen before. Turn on your TV and watch news from the other side of the world; pick up your smart phone and instantly speak to anyone, almost anywhere.

The Art of Living in the 21st century has embraced interaction and connectivity. For most of us, basic needs are readily available. For those of us who still struggle for basic needs – victims of natural disasters, despotic leaders, and pervasive poverty - your talents, skills, and creativity is needed more than ever to bring joy to yourself, humanity, and the neighbor next door.

Happiness, pleasure, connections, and great experiences are tinged with global threats like climate change, war, and conflict.

It's how we deal with it that counts.

Perhaps the most important aspect of the Art of Living in the 21st Century is the creative expression of your positive talents, skills, and communications. It energizes and empowers you; inspires you to feel alive and more connected in our complex Digital Age.

> Dance like no one is watching
>
> Sing like no one is listening
>
> Love like you're never been hurt
>
> Live like it's heaven on Earth.
>
> *Mark Twain*

How do you find your creativity?

It's really easy because it's always been with you. Think about what you like and love. Think about moving yourself into a happy, positive, and creative place. Look at the two charts on the following pages, *Where's your creativity?* Circle the words that best describe what you love to do or how you love to play. If the word isn't there, write it in the blank boxes under *"what else appeals to you?"* Keep in mind that creativity is about positive experiences – anything that harms you or someone else is negative. You want to soar – not the opposite.

This is your personal record for the art of living today.

Where's your creativity?

**fund raising
gardening
beading
quilt making
letter writing**

**painting
problem solving
sketching
cooking
sports**

**numbers
crocheting
wood working
singing
photography**

**technology
decorating
making music
yoga
travel**

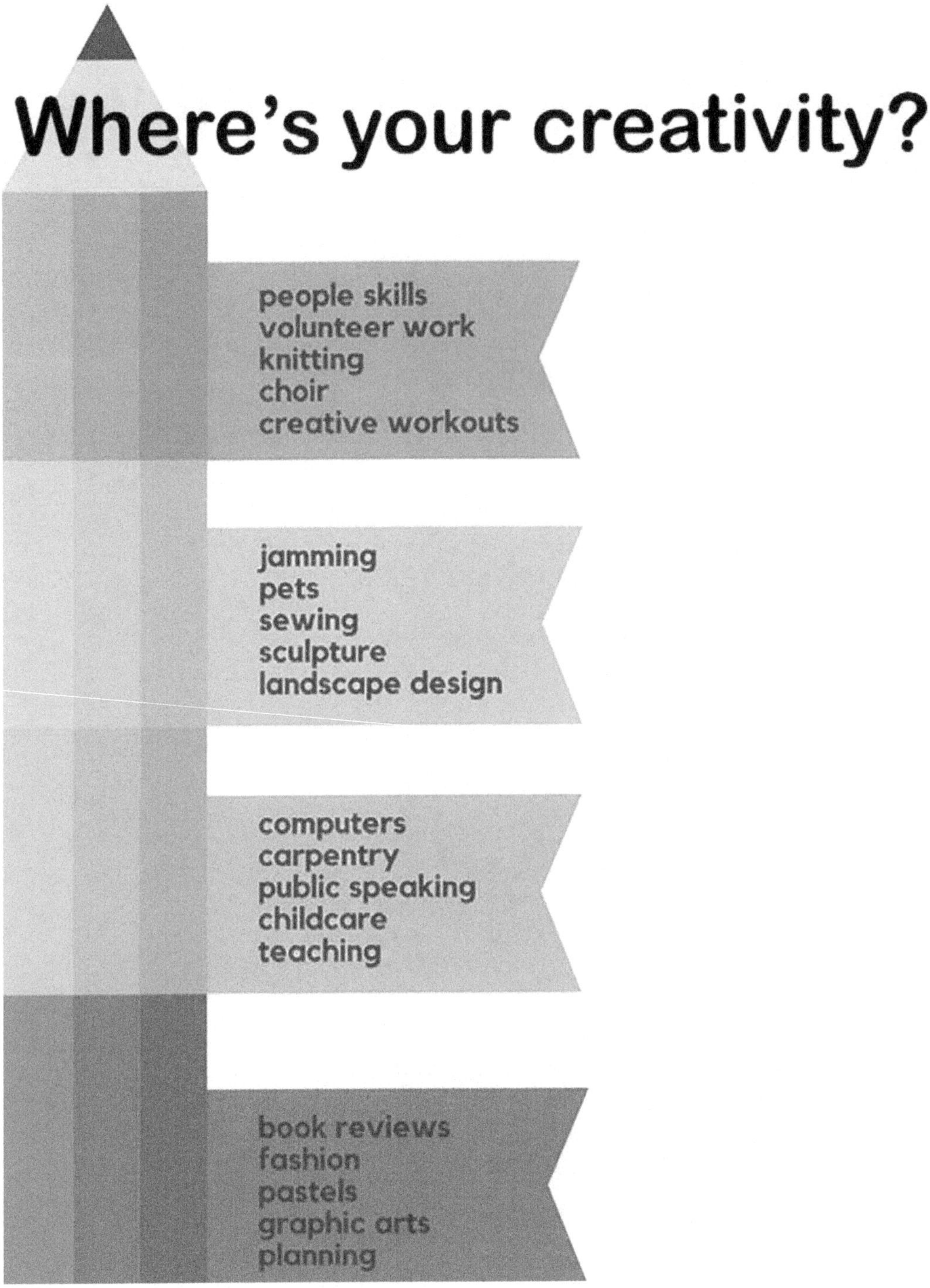

Where's your creativity?

people skills
volunteer work
knitting
choir
creative workouts

jamming
pets
sewing
sculpture
landscape design

computers
carpentry
public speaking
childcare
teaching

book reviews
fashion
pastels
graphic arts
planning

What else appeals to you?

Art of Living in The Cloud

**Join an online group that focuses
on your creative interests**

**Shop online for unique or hard-to-get tools
related to your creative interests**

**Check out images of nature, places,
people, and objects that trigger your imagination**

**Choose a famous person who represents your
creative interests (such as a chef, artist,
or designer) and study their work**

**Take an online quiz to help discover your
best creative skills**

Find an online "muse" who inspires you

Play creatively online!

**Watch YOU TUBE videos to learn different
creative techniques**

4

Rapport

> Man is by nature a social animal. Separation from others increases our need to belong.
>
> *Aristotle, 384 B.C – 322 B.C.*

You probably have five to eight close friends (and many casual acquaintances). On social media, you might have an average 350 Facebook friends and 208 Twitter followers. You can choose to join millions of different groups and sites online, reflecting every interest, hobby, or cause you can imagine.

Humans are social critters like wolves in a pack, elephants in a herd, or birds in a flock. Few of us are loners like bears and wildcats who only come together to mate or care for offspring.

People need to belong; be included with others who share similar ideas, pleasures, and pastimes. Casual social relationships help us find greater joy and meaning in life. Human "packs" are everything from a few friends having coffee, a formal club, or a well-established organization. Our natural "packs" are drawn from culture, family, and community.

You might belong to informal and special interest groups, gaming and sports groups, or fun and recreational groups. There are endless choices among the over seven billion people on the planet.

There is only one caveat.

To belong – have casual social connections, feel part of something greater than yourself, and be validated by others - requires *rapport.*

What is rapport?

Rapport is the ability to have friendly, easy relationships with others. You see rapport in the happiest player in your card playing group, the most helpful member in your hiking club, or the one everyone loves in your cooking class. Rapport comes naturally while others need to work at it.

Whether it's with one or two people, the staff at your local post office, or a well-established organization, you need to practice good social skills that connect, not separate, you from others.

There will always be people you don't agree with, others who disrupt rapport, and the loud, intrusive individual who wants to be top dog. How you respond to them is important to maintaining rapport.

Sometimes you just have to go with the flow.

Five positive results of good rapport

1. Good feelings that promote well-being
2. Pleasure in connecting and socializing with others
3. Increased creativity and productivity, especially in team efforts
4. Feeling better about yourself and/or your problems
5. Enthusiasm and increased energy

Rapport basics

The most important thing in developing rapport is motivation - asking yourself whether you want it! Do you want to join a mountain climbing group, photography club, or art class? You don't have to be perfect, just 'good enough.' If you don't like playing cards, a bridge club is not the best choice; if you're tone deaf you probably won't enjoy being in a choir; if you hate sewing then making a friendship quilt is not a great pick.

Once you find the right group, good rapport begins with being non-judgmental and looking for the positive in others. If someone is different, honor their differences; respect others for who they are, no better or worse than you. It's like arguing over the perfect chocolate chip cookie. Crispy or soft, nuts or chocolate chunks – everyone has an opinion and everyone should be heard.

If you have difficulty seeing the good side of people ask whether you're stuck in a rigid agenda. Are you willing to suspend the agenda in order to connect with people who may or may not share your views? You might learn something. Think about the old Yiddish proverb:

All of us are crazy in one way or another.

Celebrate those differences! What would our lives be like without bagels and tacos? What would our lives be like without people who wear jeans and people who wear suits? What would our lives be like without white, black, red, and brown? Nature has designed every human to be totally unique. It would be boring if we were all the same.

The art of rapport

Rapport is not about intimate relationships but friendly, casual social connections.

> **Question:** Do you know why you have two ears and only one tongue?
>
> **Answer:** Because you're supposed to listen twice as much as you talk.

Consider the following images. What do they mean? Do you practice what they say?

Listen . . . don't just hear. There's a lot going on.

Be positive. It connects you with others.

Understand non-verbal rapport/body language. There's a lot being said without words.

Ask about others, just don't talk about yourself. Volunteer in local groups and organizations. *Care.*

What would you do?

Imagine you're seeking rapport with a new group. Circle the things you think are socially appropriate.

1. Smile at everyone
2. Frown at everyone
3. Ignore it when people say negative things
4. Make fun of people
5. Compliment others
6. Try to get control of the group
7. Establish a dress code
8. Don't listen to small talk or chat
9. Ask questions about individuals
10. Decide who you like by the way they dress
11. Decide who you don't like by their hairstyles
12. Avoid people with different ideas
13. Choose who you will like and not like without any talk
14. Recognize what interests others
15. Greet everyone
16. Make quick judgment calls
17. Snub people who don't agree with you

Answers

1, 3, 5, 9, 14, 15 will help you establish good rapport!

Rapport in The Cloud

Join an online group of like-minded people

Become active in an online charitable or
social service group

Praise or compliment others in social media

If you don't have something good
to post, say nothing

Ignore trolls - they always want to start
trouble and destroy rapport

Show friends and followers that you're
positive and upbeat

Develop a website or email list of positive,
healthy people and ideas looking for
rapport in the cloud

Use a lot of LOL, :-), and other positive
icons that make people feel good

5

Insight

Who do you see in the mirror?

Insight is when you really *look* - and understand who is there. Who are you? What does your reflection say?

Insight comes with the understanding and appreciation of yourself - replacing negatives with positives. Insight means being your own friend and offering kindness to yourself so you can be kind to others.

Consider two very different women. They dress in their favorite clothes, spend time with their hair and makeup, then go to a party. Both receive many positive, sincere compliments.

The first women says happily to herself, "I really look good. I feel good."

The second woman says to herself, "Are they complimenting me because I look bad most of the time?" Which one is you?

Insight means *you know who you are*

Try this. Look in the mirror and ask yourself the following questions. Be truthful – no one is listening.

1. Is the face in the mirror happy?
2. What feelings do you see?
3. What good qualities are there?
4. Is there a reflection of another, beloved face?
5. Is there a special memory that makes you smile?
6. Do you have a rosy future?
7. Can you smile at yourself?
8. Can you laugh with yourself?

The truth about *YOU*

Guess what? You're not perfect!

Nature has designed each human to be unique – even identical twins have differences. You face different challenges, experience different joys, and have different feelings. Your environment may change and the effect can be dramatic. Your choice of significant others is unique, with potential to substantially influence your options.

Now reconsider the reflections in *your* mirror. There's a story with you as the main character. Sometimes it's in the moment – a smile for a bright sunny day or a frown for a gray, gloomy sky. Sometimes there's stress in your eyes or sadness on your face. Sometimes there's joy.

> The search for Insight is in your reflection.

Think of those two women at the party. The first woman had a solid, positive view of herself. She enjoyed the compliments because it validated her self-worth. The second woman had a dark, negative view of herself. The compliments were seen as judgmental, reinforcing her self-condemnation.

Where do you stand? Do you judge yourself harshly, refusing to see the good? Do you always look to blame yourself? Do you get angry or frustrated because you don't earn millions of dollars or wield power over others?

Insight is also about making peace, recognizing who you *are* and *are not*, and being your own friend.

Insight with a dose of reality

Often we find ourselves in that iconic space between a rock and a hard place.

We've all been there. We're all vulnerable. Insight empowers you to negotiate pain, disappointment, anger, and frustration with yourself. It also empowers you to accept yourself and your vulnerabilities, connect, and understand others.

Insight makes you SOAR.

How to develop Insight

You have to want it!

We all know people who go through life, blissfully unaware of themselves and their effect on others. If you want to be different - develop insight, connect with the real you, and accept your vulnerabilities – it's possible. It requires thought, self-examination, and befriending yourself.

Insight is the best way to identify who you are, your emotions, and select an inner path that supports well-being.

> A man [woman] should look for what is and not for what he thinks should be.
>
> *Albert Einstein*

Eight Ways to Find INSIGHT

1. INSIGHT is about knowledge and understanding of the inner self. Look inside YOU, observe your thoughts and behaviors, and be intuitive without judgment or blame.

2. Take time to nurture INSIGHT. Try meditation, mindfulness, quiet walks, visualization, deep relaxation - anything that works for you..

3. Observe and understand your inner self.

4. Avoid quickie expressions, meaningless assumptions, and simplistic self-help. True INSIGHT is a gift from you to you.

5. Don't rush things - it takes time and patience to develop understanding, knowledge, and new ways of thinking.

6. Look or think about things and ask yourself what you see and feel. Delve inside to understand your responses

7. Work in the present - the here and now.

8. Use your INSIGHT to connect with others.

Insight in The Cloud

Goggle *images of nature*. Look at the photos and
note what appeals to you the most.
Ask yourself why? What do your choices
say about you?

Google *travel images*. What apeals to you
the most? Would you like to travel there?
Why? What do your choices say about you?

Take a personality test online. Make sure it's
based on good research not silly pop ideas.

Try guided meditation, deep relaxation, or
visualization exercises online.

Experiment with color tests online. Color
preferences can show personality and character
strengths that you can explore.

Connect with others looking to develop
Inisght. You can share online ways to learn more
about yourself.

6

N OW

Live in the NOW!

There's only one way to experience life in the moment. Hit the pause button.

Why is it hard to hit pause?

Our lives are filled with moments that race by so quickly we have little time to notice. Trying to relax can be overwhelming – most of us choose from over 190 cable TV channels and 600 Hollywood movies each year. You might be one of 47 million people attending live theater or 18.1 million listening to a symphony concert or opera. That's before you count the 850 million people who go to museums, major league sporting events, and theme parks.

We're swamped with daily activities – family, work, friends, and colleagues. Our time is filled with obligations, responsibilities, family events, gaming, music, work projects, community demands, technology, clothes, food . . . the list is endless.

What happens when I pause?

It's not easy to hit the pause button and focus on the moment. When you do, life looks different. You might find beauty in a dull environments magic that was missed because you were distracted or rushed. Charm can hide in the tiniest corners; calm, if only for a moment, is there for the taking. Even when you face obstacles in health, weather, finances, and other issues, there's still room to pause.

Maybe you'll see a vivid flower on a stained glass window, a tree growing from a concrete hole on a city street, or a pigeon contemplating its world. Pause and *look*.

All we have is this moment, all we have is now . . . we link past, present, and future, all in the present moment.

Mind: A Journey To The Heart Of Being Human by Daniel J. Siegel, MD

See a butterfly. Hear the whisper of its wings.

Beauty can pop up in the most unexpected places when you're on pause.

When you take that moment

It reminds you that life is beautiful

You recall your blessings

You know that the sun will shine tomorrow

Your energy is replenished

Your concentration is improved

You appreciate the here-and-now

It reduces stress

It improves mental and physical health

You understand that NOW is available to everyone

It resets your life

Circle the most appealing ways to bring you into NOW

Walk your dog in a peaceful place

Focus on one thing that makes you feel good (don't multitask)

Live mindfully (nonjudgmental, in the present)

Do Yoga

Practice mindful meditation

Spend time in nature

Go for a slow walk on a trail or tree-lined street

Take a "compassion break" and repeat positive statements about yourself

Go fishing!

Listen to your favorite music

Make music

Garden on a beautiful day

Walk on the beach or boardwalk

Sing joyously

Exercise happily

Dance with delight

Stargaze

Find shapes in the clouds

Have fun with your kids

Have fun with your grandkids

Watch the waves on the beach

Cook something you love

Try a new hobby

Look at the local wildlife

Life may not be the party we hoped for,

but while we are here we might as well dance.

Anonymous

NOW In The Cloud

Watch animal web cams

Look at pleasing photos

Try guided meditation or relaxation online

Watch YouTube Videos that make you laugh

Take a mindfulness course

Look at photos of nature

Follow Yoga online

**Take an online seminar or workshop
that makes you feel good**

Listen to your favorite music

Look at beautiful, peaceful art

7

Gratitude

Thanksgiving is America's second favorite holiday (Christmas is Number One). 88% of Americans eat turkey that day – a total of 46 million birds consumed. Presidents "pardon" a turkey or two while nearly 50 million people travel to "give thanks" with loved ones.

In 1789 George Washington made November 26 a day of "public thanksgiving and prayer." In 1863 President Abraham Lincoln said we should count our blessings, designating the last Thursday in November as a national holiday, in the "midst of a civil war of unequaled magnitude and severity."

> If the only prayer you said in your whole life was 'thank you,'
> that would suffice.
>
> *Meister Eckhart, German theologian, philosopher, and mystic, 1260-1328*

Thanksgiving is a day of gratitude. It's celebrated around he world from turkey and pumpkin pie in the U.S. to mooncakes in China, and Yams in Ghana. Food, family, and friends – even the Macy's Thanksgiving Day Parade - is all about counting blessings not burdens.

Gratitude is thanksgiving all year 'round – a celebration of life whether you're giving or receiving. It's one of the oldest and most powerful human emotion - hard to measure or define. We all know what gratitude is and as our celebration of Thanksgiving shows, we all can own it.

Gratitude is an emotional, spontaneous response or attitude that values what you have, or can give, to make life richer and more fulfilling. It's at the heart of who you are, what and who you love, and your appreciation for life. It doesn't have to be big or small, formal or spontaneous, analyzed or impulsive.

You just have to *care.*

> When I'm worried and I can't sleep
>
> I count my blessings instead of sheep
>
> Irving Berlin, 1954

Eight things that happen when you count blessings not burdens

Life looks different when you feel gratitude. Even when things are dark, there's always some way to find gratitude. Research has shown that the benefits of gratitude range from good social development to positivity. Below are eight examples.

1. Gratitude gives you a sense of wonder

2. Awe replaces mediocrity

3. Grace enters your life

4. It's comforting

5. You appreciate what you have *not* what you don't have

6. It increases well-being

7. It improves health

8. Gratitude builds positive energy that lowers cholesterol and blood pressure

What does giving or receiving gratitude feel like?

Circle the following statements that show gratitude:

1. A child thanks you for teaching him things that are important in the world – like how to behave in a nice restaurant and smile at other people.

2. The boss ignores your hard work.

3. You let an elderly person go ahead of you on the supermarket line and there's no thank you or smile.

4. Your friend goes out of the way to help you decide which job to take.

5. Someone you care about makes an unexpected visit.

6. A colleague saves a seat for you.

7. An old friend snubs you at a reunion.

8. Someone comforts you.

9. A guest tells you how much he or she hates your cooking.

10. A neighbor doesn't thank you for taking in the mail while they're on vacation.

11. A friend takes you for a quiet walk in a beautiful place.

12. A partner surprises you with a thoughtful gift.

13. A child says he hates the gift you bought for him.

14. A neighbor brings you a dish of your favorite home-made cookies.

15. You receive a note complaining about your house from a neighbor.

16. A stranger sends you a note about how much you helped the community.

17. A friend ignores you when you need to talk.

18. A co-worker thanks you for listening.

Answers: The statements that show gratitude are: 1, 4, 5, 6, 8, 11, 12, 14, 16, 18

How to make Gratitude Your Attitude

A *gratitude attitude* is about practicing the habit of positively viewing life. Even when things look dark, if you feel surrounded by problems, and solutions seem to dangle out of your reach, a gratitude attitude helps pull you through the struggles. It's like playing Middle C on the piano, centering and balancing you in the moment. The music is always there.

Keep in mind, the more you do it the more natural it becomes. Make gratitude a habit!

Here are a few ways to develop the habit of gratitude attitude.

1. Start a gratitude journal

2. Before you go to sleep think of 3 things you're grateful for

3. Design a beautiful day that is possible and review what makes you grateful

4. Spend time with yourself to discover things around you that inspire you to feel grateful

5. Look inside yourself and be grateful for your strengths

6. Think about someone you're grateful for having in your life

7. Think about someone you love

8. Recall a time when you were honored – appreciated - by others

9. Recognize your blessings

10. Develop a daily habit of telling a spouse partner, or friend, something you appreciate about them

11. Write a letter or email to tell someone how grateful you feel to have them in your life

12. Pay attention to the people, things, and places that make you feel grateful.

If you've forgotten the language of gratitude, you'll never be on speaking terms with happiness.

C. Neil Strait, author, 1934-2003

The Science of Gratitude

Dr. Robert Emmons, one of the leading scientific experts on gratitude, defines it as a "social emotion." He views gratitude as a way to strengthen relationships "because it requires us to see how we've been supported and affirmed by other people."

Emmons' theories have been repeatedly validated by researchers all over the world. The emotion has been found to increase neural sensitivity in the medial prefrontal cortex – the part of the brain associated with learning and decision making. Simply put, the habit of expressing gratitude has the potential for lasting effects on the brain.

The power of gratitude is far reaching, affecting physical, psychological, and social behaviors. Researchers have found that people who count their blessings are happier, more optimistic about the future, and can cope better with stress and daily problems. Several studies suggest that it also decreases the risk of depression and addiction.

Emmons highlights why gratitude is so powerful for well-being:

1. Gratitude empowers you to appreciate the here-and-now
2. Gratitude can block negative emotions like envy, resentment, and regret
3. Gratitude enables you do deal better with stress
4. Gratitude helps you build self-esteem

What are you waiting for? Make thanks-giving every day and SOAR!

**"Well thank you for calling to say something positive.
We don't get a lot of that in tech support."**

Gratitude in The Cloud

Stay away from trolls

Respond to good things people send you

Compliment people online

Check out inspiring online lectures

Download a gratitude app

Write a positive review

Send a positive email or text to someone you appreciate

Download a gratitude workbook or app

Express your gratitude by forwarding, reposting, or retweeting special uplifting stories that make everyone feel thankful

We thank you for reading this book

and joining us in the journey to SOARING

Mary Ann Hannon, Dr. Jeri Fink,

and Donna Paltrowitz

Read cutting-edge Book Web Minis

Book Web Minis are fun, fast, and hot. Mini books (50-70 pages long) explore up-to-the-minute facts, photos, content, and quizzes to make you the pro. Share with friends, family, and colleagues. Don't wait – get them from Amazon.com.

Bestselling Titles:

Paranormal Is My Normal
Selfies: Picture Perfect
Timepieces: Yesterday's Stories Today
PocketCash: Your Way
Photo Power: Hidden Stories

www.bookwebminis.com

Check out Book Web Fiction

Amazon #1 Bestsellers!

Page turners bursting with haunted family trees, strange lovers, chilling photo insights, and twisted psychopaths burst into life. *Broken Books* reinvent the thriller – blending fact, fiction, and photos into riveting stories you'll never forget. Go to amazon.com to purchase these bestsellers in eBook, print (black & white), and collector's edition (full color print).

Contemporary thrillers:

Broken By Truth (Book 1)

Broken By Birth (Book 2)

Broken By Evil (Book 3)

Don't miss Book Web Historical Fiction

Go back in time to discover how good and evil thrived in the past. Meet the ancestors of the characters in the first three *Broken Books* and follow their legacy.

*Broken By Madness (*Book 4, Dutch New Amsterdam, 1654)

Broken By Men (Book 5, Spain and Portugal, 1490s)

Broken By Kings (Book 6, Sao Tome, Africa, 1494)

Broken: The Prequel (Book 7, Spanish Inquisition, 15th century)

www.hauntedfamilytrees.com

Links

Mary Ann Hannon: jazz71065@aol.com

Dr. Jeri Fink: jeri@jerifink.com

Donna Paltrowitz: donnapaltrowitz@gmail.com

Bookweb Minis: www.bookwebminis.com

Bookweb Fiction: www.hauntedfamilytrees.com

Photo Insights (original "feel-good" photos delivered weekly, for free, into you email box): http://hauntedfamilytrees.com/landing-page